Blooming
FOR
CHRIST

Growing Godly Intimacy

Barbara A. F. Brehon

WESTBOW
P R E S S®
A DIVISION OF THOMAS NELSON
& ZONDERVAN

WestBow Press books may be ordered through booksellers or by contacting:

WestBow Press
A Division of Thomas Nelson & Zondervan
1663 Liberty Drive
Bloomington, IN 47403
www.westbowpress.com
844-714-3454

Interior Image Credit: Barbara A. F. Brehon

ISBN: 978-1-9736-9976-7 (sc)
ISBN: 978-1-9736-9977-4 (hc)
ISBN: 978-1-9736-9978-1 (e)

Library of Congress Control Number: 2023909845

Print information available on the last page.

WestBow Press rev. date: 06/09/2023

Balloon plant (platycodon grandifloras) blooming for Christ! One plant, yet in different growth stages at the same time. We grow, or blossom in phases.

CONTENTS

PREFACE

The cover picture is a blooming balloon plant in my backyard. It depicts various growth stages in one image. The perennial balloon-like flower buds puff up before bursting open. The five-pointed petals of its mature blossoms are a fabulous display of God's handiwork. Each petal has tiny veins that remind me of human veins transporting life-flowing energy from the Lord, nurturing as it flows.

Balloon pistil and veins

Like the balloon plant, Christians grow, or blossom, in stages. It is one plant, yet it is in different phases at the same time. While gardening, I usually giggle with God as I ponder the complexities of simple things. Like many people, before pandemic moments, I previously took some things for granted. I thought I had a decent relationship with the Lord, yet I yearned for more intimate intimacy. I keep moving from discipleship (personal Bible study) to deeper relationship (meditation) to more intimacy (worship), toward maturity in potent worship through simple pleasures, like gardening.

Landscape redesigning turned into worship.

I often found myself in worship through writing to cope with mandated sheltering in place while recovering from an injury. The result is *Blooming for Christ*.

What started this was asking myself how the yard looked the year before. I compared pictures from one year to another. Next thing I knew, God was showing me an evolution, spiritual growth stages analogous to my balloon plants. I experienced intense worship in those moments. I can worship the Lord through deadheading faded blossoms and writing. How do you worship the Holy One?

From the week I started battling COVID in January 2022, Jesus has been pulling me closer to his bosom, into more intimacy with him, refining not redefining my call to ministry. Zion is calling me to a higher place of praise with a better understanding of the church without walls. The Lord has escorted me to totally release control of following tradition for tradition's sake to burst forth, to bloom for Christ.

We are good stewards of what we have learned, of what the Lord has entrusted to us. We must follow the Christ.

PROLOGUE

Throughout all stages of growth, our divine Creator is at work. Therefore, Christians must persevere. When we accept Christ, our individual spiritual timelines begin. The growth cycle starts with a seed that is developed. Next, germination takes place as a seed transforms into a seedling and we grow. The growth process continues with a seed germinating into a young plant that blooms. The growth cycle continues with sharing your faith experiences, which reproduces more faith. We transport our beliefs, creating lifestyles that transfer our core values to others. Wherever we go, people can recognize Christ living within us. The movement occurs with urgency to be productive and to spread seeds according to God's plan. A mature Christian is the ultimate stage to this whole process as God's harvester in preordained gardens.

Scriptural references in *Blooming for Christ*

Old Testament

Genesis 1:2

1 Kings 19:3–6

2 Chronicles 33:10–13

Nehemiah 4:15–18

Psalm 1:3

Psalms 46:10

Psalms 51:1–19

Psalm 100:5

Psalms 119:25, 28, 37, 74, 107, 114, 116

Ecclesiastes 3:1–2

Isaiah 8:16

Jeremiah 1:3–12

Jeremiah 17:7–8

Ezekiel 47:12

New Testament

Matthew 9:36–38

Matthew11:11

Matthew 14:23

Matthew 16:16–18

Matthew 28:19–20

Mark 6:46

Luke 8:1–3

Luke 16:10

INTRODUCTION

There are three books in this trilogy.

- *Reach Me with SMILES: A Handbook for Developing Disciple Makers* (2005, 2014)
- *Beyond Discipleship to Relationship: Developing Intimacy with God* (2014)
- *Blooming for Christ: Growing Godly Intimacy* (2023)

Reach Me with SMILES recognizes that Christ is the center of all teaching, and learners are the second priority. Using an acronym, it answers one question: *How does one teach a Bible lesson that will assist believers with spiritual growth?* The answer is with S M I L E S. To assist believers with spiritual growth, one must **S**timulate, **M**otivate, **I**nvolve, **L**ove, **E**ncourage, and **S**trengthen all believers. Teachers deliver the Word of God to learners so that they grow, or mature, spiritually.

The SMILES concept is recommended for teacher development to improve existing skills. It could be used independently or with groups. SMILES considers preparation for teaching as a process.

SMILES is a resource that will keep lessons fresh as you remain equipped and updated with what God has called you to do. The book offers suggestions to help teachers self-evaluate regularly and have confidence. There are processes we can use to equip disciples to make disciples of others. Furthermore, there is a distinction between "disciple" and "disciple maker" as a part of increasing effectiveness. There is a need for individuals to become more mature Christians. Therefore, let us encourage disciples to be intentional about teaching others how to demonstrate their faith.

MOVING BEYOND DISCIPLESHIP

The word *disciple* is used once in the Old Testament and more than two hundred times in the New Testament (Isaiah 8:16, Matthew, Mark, Luke, John, Acts, 1 Corinthians, and Galatians). The phrase "make disciples" is used once in the Bible in Matthew 28:19–20.

What is a disciple? A disciple is a follower, a learner, a student.

What is discipleship? Discipleship is the process of learning to be a follower of Jesus Christ. It involves building a personal *relationship* with Jesus that requires time studying the Word of God, praying to God, and exercising your spiritual gifts.

What is a disciple maker? A disciple maker is one who teaches others the things that Jesus commanded and how to observe them.

How do you make disciples? Teach them! Teach them to

observe the things commanded by God. Disciples share the Word of God and produce fruit. As you exercise your gift, you produce fruit of the spirit (Galatians 5:22–23). An apple tree produces apples. A pear tree produces pears. A fig tree produces figs. A disciple maker produces other disciples (John 15:4–8). Disciple makers help others see their need to be in growing *relationships* with God.

What is the difference between discipleship and disciple making? Discipleship is personal and occurs when an individual has decided to follow a model or set of beliefs. Disciple making involves teaching others. It happens when an individual is intentional about helping others to not only choose to be followers but also to grow.

The purpose for *Beyond Discipleship to Relationship* is to inspire individual intimacy with the Lord. Many Christians initially decided to follow Jesus seriously while meeting in small, intimate groups of people with whom they were familiar. Anyone who wants to grow and wants to help others grow in the Lord can replicate this practical approach. This book is for anyone interested in a more intimate relationship with Christ. I encourage Christians to revitalize themselves by imitating the gospel story so that others will see Christ in their lives. This developmental approach will nudge them toward spiritual growth and nurturing partnerships. Readers will be motivated to become more involved in ministries, and the church universal will grow from the inside out.

Christians must accept responsibility for their growth. Peter ends his second letter by telling us to grow in grace and knowledge of our Lord and Savior Jesus Christ (2 Peter 3:18). I know that this grace is God's special gift. Divine God allows us to walk in favor. When our souls are at peace, we position ourselves for intimacy with the Lord. Our focus shifts from the concerns that made us seek comfort to the need for divine direction each minute of the day. We can move beyond discipleship to a deeper relationship with the Lord when we sit with him regularly to learn his ways, and then practice them. The individual disciple transitions through stages of personal growth, spiritual mentoring and leadership that helps others grow, ultimately maturing as Christians.

Beyond Discipleship to Relationship addresses a discipling dilemma. Explore a process of nurturing people into active involvement in various ministries. Nurture growth when providing individual connections to the body of believers with healthy relationships that move from discipleship to a more intimate relationship with the Lord.

The process begins with a *disciple-maker*, who effectively shares his or her faith. When a person who has been affected by the disciple-maker becomes a believer in Jesus Christ as his or her personal Savior, this person becomes a *disciple*. When the disciple brings a person to Christ, the disciple-maker takes on the role of a *coach* and the disciple takes on the role of disciple-maker, thus forming a *triad*. The relationship between the original coach and disciple-maker continues, creating a cycle with a spiraling effect, and the kingdom of God increases.

Spiritual growth produces an urgency to reproduce

discipleship in others. Limited spiritual growth causes spiritual stagnation. A spiritually stagnant body of believers moves around and around in a circle. A church that is growing spiritually experiences spiraling rather than circling.

My spiritual growth makes me a work in progress; I am ever evolving, spiraling, and forever growing.

Blooming for Christ is not something that you talk about; it is something that you do. We balloon for God. As we blow up in Christ, we blow out into other people's lives for the Lord. Then, the Holy Spirit blows the breath of life into what we are doing because what we are doing is a way of expressing godly love. God makes it blossom and grow. God is the only one who can do this. It is crucial for Christians to realize inside ourselves that we can do nothing apart from the Lord. We do not make the seed grow. God's concepts are so awesome and so powerful.

LIFE CYCLE OF SPIRITUAL GROWTH

The cycle of spiritual growth is no different from that of a plant. Throughout all growth stages, God is at work and in charge. The stages of blooming or blossoming include the seed, germination, growth, reproduction, pollination, and seed spreading.[1] David, Jeremiah, and Ezekiel tell us to be like trees planted by the water growing in their seasons. This implies that God's servants must

---

[1] "The Stages of the Flower Life Cycle," Ava's Flowers, accessed June 17, 2022, https://www.avasflowers.net/the-stages-of-the-flower-life-cycle.

grow, be productive, and bear fruit (Psalm 1:3, Jeremiah 17:7–8, Ezekiel 47:12).

While blossoming, I want to cultivate the biblical types of relationships that foster my spiritual growth. God has blessed me with multiple triads for different situations or circumstances in life. I enjoy the Lord's diversity within several triad relationships. God partnered me with people who listen to me and walk with me. Depending on the situation, I might need Phoebe, Anna, Joanna, and Susanna. At other times, I might need Peter, James, and John. Furthermore, within no two triads are the same individuals, yet each individual is a rooted and grounded disciple in Christ.

Once, a pastor stated that Jeremiah trusted God below the surface to the roots. He clarified that above the surface, conditions may be stormy, or one may face blazing heat. Yet, blessings will abound with endurance rather than anxiety. Through every phase in life, we will prosper in due season if we do not wither under the stresses and pressures of a day.

We will all eventually become chaff and will exist in spirit because our earthly seasons will end. In the meantime, bloom where you are planted.

CHAPTER ONE
SEED

T he growth cycle starts with a seed; every seed holds a miniature plant.

Seeds are the small parts produced by plants from which new plants grow. In a flowering plant, three parts work together to help a seed develop and grow into a new plant. Similarly, people cannot grow without assistance in the right conditions.

When we walk with those who are similar to us in relationship with the Lord, we can share and grow within the inner circle, the triad. God has blessed me with multiple triads for different situations or circumstances in life. I like to call them my Peter, James, and John. Those were the intimate co-laborers with Christ, though he had other disciples as well. I have learned to walk in silence and seek God in my planning. This helps me to stay focused and let God lead. God will supply the seed to the sower, and will multiply what that seed produces (2 Corinthians 9:10). Who will get the glory? God is glorified; he guides us, and we must never stop growing into whatever is spiritually germinating or sprouting for our next assignment.

While God is planting seeds, so is his enemy. We must be aware of who is planting what in our gardens. Whether weak or strong, we must be vigilant as we work for the Lord. God created each of us for a purpose and implanted a mission the enemy wants to deter. Guard against allowing someone to superimpose thoughts. Others can unknowingly misdirect you with comments or suggestions.

People have ways of assuming that your situation in life is like theirs. We can superimpose their fears, ideologies, expectations, and so forth in any circumstance. However, their realities and perceptions do not necessarily make it so. For example, I was in a situation where the other person insisted on superimposing his view on me when it did not fit how I am. Just because it was real from his perspective did not mean it must be real for me. That is not my story; it was his and I respect that we were planted in different soil and sprouted differently. Simply pursue Christ. Try to follow the Lord's lead. Then, just be his mouthpiece daily by living the Jesus way. Love—do not hate people or feel negatively about the little details.

An infant balloon plant from the nursery.

POINT TO PONDER

Are you sitting where God wants? Are you moving the way God wants in this season?

Pandemic times nurtured my spiritual growth and helped me to understand that the Lord had not changed the assignment given to me more than twenty years ago. In these changing times, the Lord planted fresh seeds within me to continue the work in a different way.

It is not pivotal because I am not switching directions or shifting. I am functioning as a disciple-maker (germinating) and as an intimately maturing Christian (growing). I am reproducing disciples for Christ as well as functioning as a discipleship pollinator, a bursting balloon for Christ, spreading seeds wherever the Lord chooses using whatever platform provided for the assigned ministry. Throughout all growth stages, God is at work and is still in charge despite the spiritual war, which is a normal part of a Christian's life cycle. Spiritual war is embedded in each stage of life, so we grow on.

HECTIC

In a spiritual war, one must be focused on spiritual things for the growth of the kingdom. The Lord reveals a lot of good bits and pieces while I sit in my Jesus chair, that spot where I ponder points and chew on God's Word. Once I dreamed about faceless people, and God later explained that the dream was not about the people or their faces. It was a message about spiritual warfare going on at that time. God prevented me from becoming entangled with a few faceless people setting traps. I was stopped from becoming overwhelmed with others planting seeds of distraction. God wanted me to replace those superimposed thoughts with walking in silence and seeking God in my planning—God's plan. The Lord did not instruct me to respond to the faceless. That was exciting! It became a-thrill-a-minute rather than hectic. Be aware of who is planting what in your garden.

The people were faceless because it was the concept that was important, not the face. Who are the distractors, and who will draw you closer to Jesus? I want to cultivate the types of relationships that are not void. I know that I need significant others who will walk with me ministering, like Joanna, the wife of Chuza, Herod's household manager, and Susanna, and many others, who provided for Jesus out of their means (Luke 8:1–3). I need the types of relationships that permeate time. Regardless of how long it has been, even a few years, it seems like we last spoke the day before.

Void and *avoid* both suggest facelessness. In a certain sense, there is a void for the average person when something or someone is no longer present in that person's life. However, in God's spiritual sense, there is not a void at all; just avoid the faceless, whom God gradually replaces. That is so critical to growing in Christ. In the words of one of my mentees, "Stop looking at the void, and avoid things that trigger you to not trust God. Speak to the places that seem empty."

I do not feel a sense of emptiness where God has decided to peel away, purge, shift, or remove people. Pruning and deadheading, or whatever you want to call it, did not leave a void because God replaced it with something else. Since the Lord has already relieved me of it, all I need to do is recognize what is already there, available for where I am headed. God provided spiritual space to see what was next and to move toward that instead of hanging on to the other.

I remember the hour-and-a-half drive one way from seminary to home one weekend. More than twenty years ago, I fervently prayed to God, "Teach me to trust you more." Now there have been countless times when the Holy Spirit has reminded me, "I'm still teaching you to trust me."

Remove extra voices to hear God's voice more clearly. Get rid of the voices in seclusion and in moments of meditation. Jesus helped me perceive that. He was at the beginning, too, and he pulled this together for me. In the beginning, the earth was void, or empty (Genesis 1:2). The Lord can speak to your empty places and fill them with things that are already available to you. God has already replaced your void with something else. Use your spiritual eyes to see it. Stay close to the Lord, abide in him, and you will experience fewer voids, becoming more effective.

To be effective for the Lord, hectic multitasking is unnecessary. I must meet the demands of the Lord rather than of people. I must serve people in the name of Jesus but not allow them to manipulate and control the direction or means for the assignment. I do not need to allow myself to be pressed to the point that I am going here and there and everywhere, becoming overwhelmed with other people's agendas and issues. Other people are important, and I must avoid the notion of "serving with a long-handled spoon." I must serve others who are a part of my divine assignment, which does not work so well from a distance. I must serve them where they are and understand that we are planted in different soil mixtures. I must love them.

Simultaneously, I must protect the use of my time to do what God chooses in divine time. I do not think that I will ever pick my pace back up to hectic. Thank you, pandemic. I realized there was no need for that pace after a very nice family reunion week. I was relaxed, retired, and still getting things done according to God's agenda. While working a full-time job, I needed to render to Caesar what belonged to Caesar. However, that is no longer my story. I gave an honest day's work for an honest day's pay. And now? Each day is for whatever God says because the Lord turned my leaf from being employed full-time to fully following God all day, planting seeds every day differently, joyfully, peacefully.

How effective was the product of multitasking? Could I have done the job better if I had limited my focus? It took me a long time to get there. Our culture, our nation, and the world tend to think that multitasking is the way that people get things done. My sister and I have questioned the effectiveness of that. I am doing my best to stop multitasking. I am using spiritual discernment to determine when to tell someone to wait. It is not always necessary to say no, however, sometimes saying, "Not now" is appropriate.

CHAPTER TWO

GERMINATION

ermination is the part of the growth process when a seed transforms into a young plant or a seedling. It sprouts its own roots, stems, and leaves. The sprout needs to be sustained and nurtured. All seeds need moisture, oxygen, and the right temperature to germinate or grow. If the seed gets too much water, it becomes soggy and rots. If it is not protected from a scorching sun, it could burn. However, when the conditions are right, it thrives with small shoots; it sprouts. Our growth in the Lord must not become stunted, scorched, or rotten.

We all need nurturing, and sometimes that is manifested in dreams. God has many ways to talk to us to help us grow. For me, a dream is a conversation with God.

Barbara A. F. Brehon

A CONVERSATION WITH GOD

In a long, interesting dream, I was at an outdoor event attended by a large group of people. I do not generally enjoy festivals or crowds of people. We visited vendors when I would rather have explored other sites. However, I waited while they did those things. I listened to comments of passersby and vendors about how long I had been in that one place despite all that was going on around me. Yet, I waited for the people with whom I had attended.

After standing around waiting for them as they did what I did not want to do, we got something to eat. I left for a moment. When I returned to the table, they were gone, their places cleared, and my place with food was just as I had left it, not even covered with a napkin.

After not eating the food, and after going off by myself at this festival-like event, I happened upon a youth event outdoors in front of my home church. It spread the whole block of the church's property. I took pleasure in seeing adults who were children when I was there. The youth sponsor was nurturing the children of today and doing so with enthusiasm and genuine care. She was smiling and satisfied by spending time doing what she was doing.

Even while dreaming, I found myself talking to God and asking him what a certain thing meant. There I was, actually having a conversation with God throughout the dream experience without having negative feelings or thoughts. Whatever I was hearing people say, whatever I was doing, whatever I was watching, I was having a conversation with God at the same time. I did not want to let the dream go until my Almighty God answered what I was asking. Then, I kept going, one situation after another connecting in the same environment.

Eventually, I was lying there, and I felt like I was awake. I felt like I was asleep at the same time. I was just having the conversation with God, but it was all part of the same scenario. It was all part of what my precious Lord was doing, having a conversation with me to nurture me for the next leg of my assignment. Of course, I did not know that at the time.

There were several lessons gleaned after awaking from the dream. God was telling me not to wait for people to do their trivial stuff that delays my ability to see all that is available right around me to experience and enjoy. Step with me and do not wait for them to finish what they are doing. Your food will get cold while you wait. They will leave you at the table to eat by yourself or leave your cold food unattended when you go to take care of what you have to do—the assignment I gave you.

It was noteworthy to dream this *after* analyzing data gathered from an event under my leadership. Moreover, I can reflect on developing and launching an app for Favored by the Father Ministries without knowing anyone in my context who had done that before. God made resources available to me during a specific season of ministry.

As I reflect on this dream, I see that I left behind the current people who were holding me back. In the dream, I mused over the past success of my early ministry. That must give me impetus into my next. I personally have let people, through their opinions, silence, and the thought of how they would feel if I failed, hold me back from many things. I have learned to walk in silence and seek God in my planning. Follow God especially when others around you do not get it. Stay focused and let God lead. When we walk amongst those who are similar to us in relationship with the Lord, we can share and grow within the inner circle, the triad. Please keep in mind that will not be a lot of people.

We receive so many hints from God through the words and messages that overflow from others. Align what you hear with God's word. The written and spoken word of God assures us that our lives will remain stable and steadfast, and become renewed and strengthened when we feel greatly afflicted or uncertain (Psalms 119:25, 28, 37, 74, 107, 114, and 116). Align what you hear with God's voice that you know you heard during your conversations with him. Try the spirit of God by the Spirit of God to stay focused and hear his lead and affirmation. I am so grateful for the inner circle, the triad that God gave me. Their messages, texts, and conversations help me grow in unimaginable ways. Therefore, a lesson learned is worth revisiting.

POINT TO PONDER

Look at God. As we grow, we know God's goodness is based on His loyal love and His truth. Psalm 100:5 says that the Lord is good and merciful, and his truth endures to all generations. How is the Lord speaking to you right now?

We all need people to balloon us with affirmations and corrections as needed so we can *bloom for Christ*. For me, this is nontraditional. I am glad God partnered me with people who listen to me without evaluating me or indulging me. My Phoebe, Anna, and John prayerfully support me as I move in the Lord regardless of stumbling blocks. I am grateful to God for placing people, events, and even dreams at just the right times to keep us rooted. I will expose my roots for divine snipping in the Lord's ordained time, but not when people choose. I am encouraged even by the words I am allowed to deliver. I was full to overflowing from the dream and from sharing it privately a few times with different intimate others, my triad.

After reflecting on the dream, just sitting with it for a bit, I could see that God was doing something new in me. One person told me, "Allow Him to use you, Dr. BB." First Corinthians 16:13–14 also tells us to be watchful, faithful, courageous, and strong while we complete our divine assignments, doing everything with love. The dream helped me to see that it is the message that matters, not the faces.

That dream was very pivotal and powerful, yet not disturbing. God gave me prayer partners plus spiritual confidants. Love people rather than hate them. Avoid feeling negatively about people and events. Simply pursue Christ, who is not going to take us where we have no business going. Christians must stop following people and follow God's lead. Then, just be his mouthpiece for a little while. Lovingly do what God says. That is it!

God is letting me know my assignment is decisive. The methods for completing the assignment are different from twenty years ago, however, the mission is the same. I am not switching directions. I am sitting where I should be sitting, moving the way I should be moving. It is in God's time and that is so encouraging and so exciting.

God does reveal things in dreams, and we bloom for him. We balloon. As we blow up in him, we blow out into other people's lives for him. Then, the Holy Spirit blows the breath of life into what we are doing because what we are doing is godly love. God is the only one who can make it grow and blossom.

Therefore, I find satisfaction in that, and the Lord is telling me to leave the other people alone. That is not the Lord telling me to dismiss them; do not fret. Germinate. Just keep moving, doing, and shedding the outer covering of your seed. Peripheral onlookers are watching in awe of God. Eventually, the Almighty will show them what they need to see. That part is not up to me. We must realize within ourselves that we can do nothing. We do not make the seed grow. God's concepts are so awesome and so powerful.

We do not know how God is going to come to us; however, prayer is answered. Yet, it does not have to be a certain way. It is a simple conversation with God. The answer might be in a dream or while you are doing your daily walk, while you are gardening, while you are doing whatever you normally do, naturally living your life each God-given day. Let it be and enjoy living life to the fullest with God. Whatever that means to you, go on doing what seems to be a little small thing. It might be with that song you cannot stop humming and singing.

CHAPTER THREE

GROWTH

Favored by the Father Ministries
Resources to help you grow

Rev. Dr. Barbara A. F. Brehon

P. O. Box 1114
Tappahannock, Virginia 23560

www.barbaraafbrehon.com

When ordering new business cards in 2021, I stumbled across the one I chose in 2014 with the same image of the plant I bought in 2020 and had never heard about.

The growth cycle starts with a seed. Germination transforms it into a young plant, the next part of the growth process. To keep growing, the seedling needs food, just like people and animals. People and animals get their food by eating it, whereas plants make their own food by using air, water, and energy from the sun; that is photosynthesis.[2] During photosynthesis, the plant makes oxygen as a waste product, which helps us breathe. The seedling plant grows through continuous cell division during the developmental period; it looks awkward or unusual compared to its mature state. During this time, plants are busy using their resources of sunlight, water, and carbon dioxide and storing resources for blooming and reproduction.

Spiritual growth is similar to a plant's growth. God plants a seed within us, and it germinates into a young, on-fire-for-the-Lord servant. To keep growing, the servant needs food, and becomes a diligent disciple, deliberately reading and studying the Word of God daily. During spiritual photosynthesis, the servant-disciple makes use of available resources and continuously multiplies his or her faith by sharing the Word and personal testimony and evangelizing for new disciples. This developmental period fosters blooming and reproduction.

When under pressure, James 1:12 helps us to better understand that we are fortunate to be able to exercise faith. Our patience with ourselves in troubling times helps us to meet challenges and endure testing and temptation when we know that God will reward those who endure for Christ's sake. I remember an Instagram post stating, "It is only when a seed is in the dark and under pressure that new life can come out of it. Then it fulfills its potential as it grows towards the light." I pray to my loving Lord

---

[2] "What happens in the seedling growth stage of germination?" BYJU'S, accessed March 1, 2023, https://byjus.com/question-answer/what-happens-in-the-seedling-growth-stage-of-germination/.

to help me be steadfast for his glory and continually push through life's pressures towards the light of Jesus. May I forever be loyally in love with sweet Jesus.

SPIRITUAL TIMELINE

I accepted my call to preach in 1995, began seminary in 1996, and was licensed to preach in May 1997. I remember feeling awkward when my spiritual father asked us to explain our calls to the ministry during a weekly ministers' training session. I had not yet started seminary. I was trying to answer his question while simultaneously listening to the Lord talk to me. This was nothing I previously considered. I was germinating.

After speaking, I pondered what I had just said and what it really meant, and I was absolutely confused. "I am going to run a church." As I write this paragraph, I am serving as associate pastor of a church, as moderator (like a president) of an association of thirty-five churches, and as visionary servant leader of Favored by the Father Ministries, a church without walls with a digital application. God plants seeds and prepares people for preordained ministry, which is not always preaching and traditional pastoring. Even this writing is ministry.

When I graduated from the School of Theology of Virginia Union University as valedictorian of my seminary class in 1999, I remember thinking, "Of whom much is given, much is required. Lord, what are you going to do to me?" I cried uncontrollably. Retrospectively, I am where my omniscient Lord knew I would be that day in ministers' training. Every experience has been compiled or synthesized to this point. My awkwardness and confusion were spiritual prickles indicating that God wanted me to think out of the box about running a church. My awkward prickles were spiritual prods pushing me to what God originally said. Having not seen it before, I misinterpreted God wanting me to "run" a church without walls.

When looking at 1996 and 1997, I see that my mindset, my experiences to date, would not allow me to receive some God-given gifts. I took spiritual gifts inventories and taught classes on that topic. I chose at the time not even to acknowledge that I had certain gifts. I wanted to have other spiritual gifts. According to a later inventory in 2001, I grew in giving, knowledge, prophecy, shepherding, discernment, and evangelism. In addition, mercy and healing strengthened a lot. In 2002, I continued to teach others about identifying and using their spiritual gifts. I commented that how I understand myself changes as I grow in Christ. That statement has a strong impact on me to this day.

Twenty years later in 2022, another group with which I am affiliated asked participants to complete a gifts assessment. I dug up the old ones to compare after I received the online results of this most recent inventory. I noted that I had acknowledged through the gifts inventory apostleship that I previously squashed. God has a way of ensuring that we fulfill our callings. These days, I do not think it matters what name or title we give to any assignment. What matters most is whether we do what God tells us to do when we are told and the way we are told.

I am still germinating; I am forever growing, shedding chaff that covers my seed. The assignments I give to myself may face endless obstacles and hurdles. However, the assignment coming from God will be completed. Isaiah 55:6–11 helps me to understand that just like rain and snow do not go back until they water the earth, God's words are not empty. Just like rain and snow complete their work, I must complete my assignment also.

After doing some exegetical work on Ephesians 2:21–22, I had a feeling that stirred to the core of my being. There was a strong urgency in me. It made me want more. It made me want to do more. I needed to make myself more available for God to use me in whatever state I am in. If I can do more, I want to do more. If I have the resources to do more, I will do more. Whatever God has allotted, appointed, and assigned, I want to accomplish in the name of Jesus. It is in him that I live, breathe, move, and have my very being (Ephesians 2:19–22; Matthew 16:18; 1 Corinthians 3:11; 1 Corinthians 3:16–17; 1 Peter 2:5; 2 Corinthians 6:14–18; 1 Timothy 3:15–16).

To balloon for Christ, you must start with a structure on a foundation into which God can pour himself. God plants the seeds in us, waters them, and they will grow. A growing Christian must be a dwelling in which God can live, breathe, and have his being in as he or she abides and has his or her being in him. You are ballooning, bursting forth, maturing. I want to increase and grow for a prolonged or sustained amount of time. I do not want my growth to be seasonal or temporary, but approved, favorable, and acceptable to the Lord. Oh God, I thank you for the indwelling, for my spiritual photosynthesis!

The more we grow, the more we know that we are not strangers or aliens to God. We are fellow citizens with Christ. Being a fellow citizen is being part of the congregation of believers, which does not necessarily indicate a specific local body that meets in a church building. We are art of the church universal, a church without walls. Our foundation has Christ as the chief cornerstone, which nothing can penetrate or overcome.

BALANCE

I have been dealing with the theme of personal balance in my life for years, and I may have to deal with that until the day I die. People can sideswipe you and people can knock you off course. If you do not have the appropriate balance, you teeter and you totter, but teetering and tottering do not mean that you fall. If you do, get back up and keep growing so that you can share that experience, and those experiences, to help others grow. Sharing your faith reproduces it.

Plants reproduce, or make more of their kind, either by seeds or spores. *Blooming for Christ* has been dealing with seeds, so I will stick with that.

I was off balance and so I had to cut things off to get the balance back. God does that for you, and tells you what to trim, which I will talk about later (trim your roots; be transplanted and trimmed).

I looked at a document I created and framed to go on the wall by my front door. It reads, "Lord, may each day be a conversation with you." God did exactly that in my dream and I could not let it go. I did not want it to end without resolution.

Have a conversation with God all day each day.

Barbara A. F. Brehon

What is the message? It was not wrestling, and it was not like a dream of entertainment. I do have dreams where I just smile, and there is not really a lesson in it; it was just enjoyment. Living in balance like that is blessed, which is a lesson. There is a time for this and a time for that, and we listen for the way God says to go. We just need to have balance.

Go where you need to go, and do what you need to do. Continue to live your life. Life is happening all around you. What others are going through at a given time does not have to draw you into a bad place. Some people are like dangerous reefs that can shipwreck you; they are like trees in the autumn that are doubly dead, for they bear no fruit and have been pulled up by the roots (Jude 1:12). However, there is nothing bad going on in your life in those moments. Express your concerns and help others to perceive where God is in any situation.

God wants people to hear someone affirm them without judgment. We follow God's guidance the best we can, yet things happen in life that knock us off balance. That is temporary. The presence of our Divine God might be working through you to escort them through the rough spot by being immovable in faith that sustains you.

Others observe you continuing to grow, ever evolving yet moving toward your created purpose. You are who you are, sharing in those difficult moments with your presence, your listening ear and your prayerful posture all bringing peace. Simply give support to others with loving kindness without falling into their temporary holes. When you both hurt, admit it and keep growing. Simply be available in various seasons and keep growing.

PARALLEL GROWTH

God lets us create balance separately but at the same time as we travel on two roads. God is feeding me content while feeding you what you need for where you are. God is having conversations with both of us, simultaneously feeding and fulfilling according to a predetermined plan, according to what each part of the triad distinctly needs. It always amazes me to consider how God is so omnipotent and omnipresent, meeting all needs at the same time. Each of us blooms for Christ separately, distinctly, simultaneously. Whatever it is that you are working on and whatever it is that you and your ministry partner are doing will intersect. Continue to travel parallel roads to the intersection. We will drive different vehicles on cruise control. Eventually we will tap the brakes because we are following God's guidance; we will not have to slam on the brakes. We will tap to disengage the cruise control, to temporarily disentangle ourselves from distractions, and we will intersect. We will pull into a parking lot, and we will go in and dine together. Something will be created so that others will be able to feast on it. Later, we will drive back to our respective gardens and continue the growth process. God clarifies with distinctiveness for each person separately, yet simultaneously. God is doing God's way. Walk with that and keep the balance. All those willing to follow will be spiritually elevated to loftier places and deeper depths. We must become more intimate with God. We must create time to worship realizing that there are multiple ways to worship.

If God already equipped you before you launch into your assignment, then all you do is stay in the way and go for it. When you need to spend money to do something, having been equipped already, you will have all the resources you need, all the oxygen you need. If it is already preordained, it is going to be. God's process to equip you includes strengthening your trust in God. As you germinate and grow, the Lord will teach you to trust more.

For example, I visited with a young lady at a restaurant because she had been working there as a waitress. I wanted to have her by myself, and we had our personal conversation. I tipped her with Cash App and told her to expect it. God let me know that I did exactly the right thing and exactly the right way. When she came back to the table to bring my bill, she said, "When I went to cash you out, somebody already took care of your bill."

I said, "Excuse me?"

"Yes, it was already paid. Somebody already took care of it."

God predetermined the chunk of change I gave her before I left the house, and I did not have to pay a dime. As I walked out, I saw someone I knew, and God identified her. I hugged my phantom philanthropist; she smiled and admitted her act of kindness, and I identified the friend to my waitress.

God has already provided the resources for each one of us to be abundantly blessed in multiple ways. Unlimited resources are already in place. You may not know how God will sponsor a podcast, but it is a great thing to admit, "God, I don't know how." Admitting is not a weakness. "Oh God, I don't know how I am going to do this." Then, confirmation comes that you are ready for your next assignment and God will show you one more piece. You will not see your next until you complete your now: what was already given you to do. Why give you more to do if you have not finished the previous assignment? Be faithful in the small things (Luke 16:10).

POINT TO PONDER

What is your incomplete assignment? Why did you pause or totally stop? Pause to pray about that now to get to your next.

CHAPTER FOUR

REPRODUCTION

As our faith matures, we will find ourselves teetering and tottering, which does not mean that we fall. If we do, we get back up and keep growing so we can share that experience, those experiences, to help others grow. Sharing our faith reproduces it.

Plants reproduce, or make more of their kind, by either seeds or spores. *Blooming for Christ* features the balloon plant, so I will concentrate on seeds.

How do balloon plants reproduce? Balloon plants self-seed quickly. Balloon flowers are productive self-sowers and can sometimes be persistent. They naturally spew out seeds from pods, transporting them throughout the garden. When the flower fades, one can see that a pod has formed at the end of a stem. Each pod contains many tiny brown seeds. To limit the potential of them overgrowing the space, practice deadheading blossoms throughout the season, removing all stems after blooming ceases. Deadheading stops self-seeding and is time consuming. Some see deadheading as a problem. I do not mind taking this time knowing it results in more blooms throughout the growing season. Another option is to give an active self-sower space to grow and reseed.

How do Christians multiply? While all balloon plants self-seed naturally, people do not self-seed. Some Christians disperse seeds and some wither. Some spread one or two seeds here and there, while others distribute far and wide. God wants us to reproduce; Jesus said to make disciples of all nations (Matthew 28:19). Overgrowing the space is not a problem because there is plenty of room in God's Kingdom. Give an active Christian sower room to grow.

Blooming for Christ illustrates discipleship, stewardship, and reproduction at the same time. Stewardship is really about maximizing available resources, which can be other people.

PREGNANT WITH POSSIBILITIES

Once, when I became unexpectedly sick, my mentee said that she was smiling and overjoyed because I was spiritually pregnant. She explained that I was in the labor room and the effects from birthing were coming forth. She went on to say it was a joy, so I should mount up with my armor. The breakthrough was on the way; it was coming forth. She concluded with the thought that we were approaching Pentecost, therefore, I should allow the Spirit to lead. That was June 3. The *Blooming for Christ* concept hit me while gardening that same year on June 16.

To backtrack a little, for no apparent reason on June 2, I regurgitated a salad that I freshly prepared. Around 5:00 p.m., I went to the bank about a debit card activation that did not happen smoothly. They closed at 4:00, so I returned home and fixed and ate a salad with ingredients I bought the same afternoon. I drank tea along with it. Less than an hour after finishing, I regurgitated *all* of it. About 7:00 p.m., after cleaning the mess up, I curled up on the couch and felt okay. My feet were on the floor at 4:30 a.m. and I started a laundry load of the splattered clothes from the night before. I then sent the daily morning message via social media to subscribers entitled "The Unchanging God." I did not ingest anything until the next morning. I sipped coffee and felt fine, just queasy.

Asking God what all that was about, I journaled the words *cleaning, purging,* and *removing.* Anything with potential to harm me was removed before it could get into my system. There was no bile taste at all before, during, or after. God fearfully and wonderfully made the human body.

I shared this with two people I consider friends, my James and John; both call me mentor. I asked them to tell me what God said to them about it after they prayed over it. The younger one responded that I was spiritually pregnant while my older friend told me, "Everything that is toxic to you, physically or spiritually, God will remove from you before it harms you. The weapon may be formed (as in the food) to poison but it will not succeed. He did his process of elimination by reversing the order and canceling what could have been different."

God uses triads to work in our lives, personally as well as in a congregation. The mentor/mentee relationship does not just go one way. We help one another grow in the Lord, reproducing Christ's work. I met my younger friend at a function with the older friend. A few years later, she asked me to mentor her, and our relationship continues to flourish. Our obedience to the Lord becomes easier, as we hold one another accountable for who and what we say we are. While those relationships grow, others develop and still others diminish. God will supply the seed and multiply it (2 Corinthians 9:7–12).

Align what you hear with God's word and God's voice. You know what you heard during your conversations with the Lord. Keep letting him feed you through intimate ministry partners. The Lord speaks to all of us with his sweet Holy Spirit; therefore, we can rely on each other to prayerfully partner with us. Then, despite moments like I had battling COVID-19 in January 2022, you can shed the chaff to stand upon the mountain and magnify the Lord's name. Words from the song permeated my spirit when I could not talk due to COVID. Tell all the people and every nation that he reigns. Zion is calling me to a higher place of praise. This is my pandemic proclamation.

Those moments were God's opportunity to pour into me, to refine my calling in a way that made it clear to use more available resources to reach people for the Lord's glory. Yes,

God deadheaded my blossoms and it hurt in many ways. Sometimes we need to have our plans thwarted and our blossoms snipped, which promotes more blossoms. It amazes me how God pruned people out of my life, thereby making room for current relationships to blossom. Pruning makes us pregnant with possibilities. What God can do through us bursts forth and discipleship shifts. Discipleship becomes intimacy; growth births deeper intimacy as we balloon and allow God to snip our blossoms.

Deadheaded balloon plant after transplanting to the front yard.

BURSTING FORTH

Having never given biological birth, God gave me fertility by producing offspring for Christ. Figurative language in scripture helped me to perceive this concept when the apostle Paul told the Galatians that he was in the pains of childbirth until the life of Christ was visible in them (Galatians 4:19, 27).

The indwelling of the Holy Spirit overpowering you from the inside makes you burst forth in praise, grow to higher heights and deeper depths as you perform the ministry preordained for you to do. It makes you want to pop until the pistil explodes. The pistil is the seed-producing part of a flower and has five parts. The stigma receives pollen to affect reproduction. The style provides a place for the pollen tube to grow and acts as a barrier for bad pollen. The pollen tube enables the pollen to go from the stigma through the style to the ovary. The ovary protects the ovules. It is the job of the ovules to fertilize the pollen to grow it into a seed. Fertilization ensures the ovule will eventually develop into a seed.[3]

POINT TO PONDER

What is the point of a pistil? It supports the pollination process, which leads to fertilization.

---

[3] https://www.homestratosphere.com/parts-of-a-flower/ Accessed 6/17/2022.

Five petals, five stigmas, five filaments, representing me:
the fifth of five children born in the fifth month.

Our spiritual pistils are full of seeds to spread. Within the life cycle of spiritual growth, I am not barren. I pray that you are not spiritually barren either.

As I preach, teach, minister, mentor, and simply try to walk in the Lord's way, I am spreading seeds like the perennial balloon plant spreads its seeds at maturity. Mature Christians must become disciple makers because the spirit of God within wells up. The resulting explosion sends seeds that need nurturing and need to be escorted through the stages of development. Every year, I find new balloon plants appearing where I did not plant, yet God provided the conditions that nurtured them for the next season. Deadheading promotes more blossoms during the growing season, so there is more seed spreading.

The larger ones grew from planting; the smaller ones of different sizes are from the parent spreading seeds.

We all need nurturing, even after reaching maturity. This nurture affects a lifestyle for Christ that easily flows in diverse triad relationships, and it propels into other relationships. I thank God every day for my multiple triad interactions.

POINT TO PONDER

Does that describe what you do for Christ?

NEXT LEVEL OF CHRISTLY INTIMACY

We must follow the Lord to recognize when methods shift but not the mission. Become more productive as good stewards of what we have learned, of what has been entrusted to us. Sometimes we must be still. Sometimes we must simply be still knowing who God is, remembering what the Almighty living Lord can do (Psalms 46:10). When we are going through tough times, all we need to do is turn to God and be honest with him, who knows all about it already.

In 1 Kings 19:3–6, Elijah was afraid and ran for his life. He was frustrated and told the Lord that he had had enough and wanted to die. God sent an angel to minister to him. When you have had enough or you are just tired, seclusion can be an appropriate response (Matthew 14:23, Mark 6:46, John 6:15). Some of us did not know how tired we really were with our circumstances until we were mandated to shelter in place because of a pandemic.

I thank God for being sovereign and for choosing whatever is necessary to get my attention and encourage me to spend more time, to become more intimate, and to become more productive.

On March 19, 2022, I prayed a solitary prayer: "Lord, I know there are times when I must come to you in prayer alone to help me recover and re-center myself in you, especially after dealing with difficulties. In Jesus's name, I humbly pray. Amen."

I felt an intensified and clarified call to minister with next level intimacy during a devotional from Psalms 51:1–19. This psalm of David, regarding the time Nathan the prophet came to him after David had committed adultery with Bathsheba, mirrored my feelings and need for more closeness with God than ever before. At some point, I believe all of us must acknowledge our wrongdoings, even if we have not committed the same wrong David committed. The remorse is real in your inward parts. Have mercy on me and do not leave me, Lord.

Convicted! God was not pleased with my whining, reluctant-to-do-and-go spirit. Forgive me, Lord. A verse often used in relation to stewardship applies here. 2 Corinthians 9:7 tells us that God does not want anything from us that we give grudgingly but only that we give cheerfully.

CHAPTER FIVE

POLLINATION

A pollinator is anything that helps carry pollen from the male part of the flower (stamen) to the female part of the same or another flower (stigma). The movement of pollen must occur for the plant to become fertilized and produce fruits, seeds, and young plants. Insects pollinate balloon plants. Some pollinators intentionally collect pollen. Others move pollen accidentally while they are drinking or feeding on nectar in the flower blooms and unknowingly transport from flower to flower.[4]

A Christian pollinator carries Jesus Christ wherever he or she goes. This movement must occur for the Kingdom of God to grow. The Christian pollinator stays busy fertilizing and producing disciples for Christ. Each carries out his or her assignment distinctly. One plants the seed, another person waters it, but God makes it grow. Each pollinator is part of this process, but God is at

---

[4] https://www.nps.gov/subjects/pollinators/what-is-a-pollinator.htm The National Park Service was accessed on August 26, 2022.

the center of the development (1 Corinthians 3:6–15). Distinctly, God has conversations with us to simultaneously transport us according to what each one needs and is supposed to do.

Some Christian pollinators intentionally collect and carry God's truth so that others anticipate or expect their coming and their delivery. Others transport God's message incidentally. While something else is going on, someone is ingesting what that pollinator drank or ate from the Bible or the Holy Spirit without the pollinator knowing it. Incidental learning happens when one is teaching one thing, yet the learner picks up other concepts or nuggets of information during that moment. The pollinator's lifestyle and conversation impart the spirit of God without a second thought. Sometimes, unknowingly, we transport from one to another. Sometimes we try too hard to make a point or to position ourselves to proclaim or teach God's word. Just live it!

DR. BB AND THE BEE

Hover bees love the balloon plant. I learned that they really do not care a thing about me. I do not need to run from the bee when I hear it buzzing around me. All I need to do is be still or move to another plant while it gets nectar from the one it chooses. When it moves to the one where I am, I can move to deadhead a different plant. The bee hovers and sucks from one plant at a time and pays no attention to me.

Unlike humans, nature does not misinterpret the Creator's intentions. For example, the hover bee does what God created it to do. Sometimes we pay more attention to our enemy when God is working through something using its own designed purpose. Then, we realize God's enemy is not doing anything. We can superimpose our thoughts, fears, ideologies, expectations, and so on in any circumstance. However, our realities and perceptions do not necessarily make it so. That bee did not care about me. She cared about getting nectar. Once I learned to respect the bee's right to function in her God-created manner for God-created purposes, I was able to enjoy sharing the same space in my garden with the bee that previously petrified me and ran me in the house. Actually, the bee did not chase me anywhere; my own perception did that.

On one occasion, a friend's perspective and mine were quite different. Neither was right or wrong, simply different, since our life experiences gave us separate perceptions of a similar circumstance. God provided the opportunity for each of us to grow in our pollination stages. We both became more effective listeners and sharers for the Lord.

What he was doing in his situation did not mirror mine, though he thought it did. I simply asked, "What are you doing that causes people to respond or not respond to you according to what you want, according to what you expect?" That was not for me to delve into. He needed to listen to the will of the Holy Spirit to take him to his next. It was not for me to push him to what I thought his next ought to be. That is huge!

At first, he was superimposing his view on me. I simply stated that I understood what he was saying but that was not my story.

When something similar happened to me, the response was about other people and was not accurate for me. What the other person shared was real for that person, but that is not how it happened for me. Just because it is real for someone else does not mean it must be real for me. That is not *my* story.

Respect your reality and respect that your experience is not necessarily someone else's story. I pray that both of us walked away as more effective Christian pollinators with intentional and incidental outcomes for the people we serve.

POINTS TO PONDER

- Do not run. Stand firmly on your God-created purpose and become a more effective Christian pollinator. I assume you know your purpose, or your function, for being, for existing. What is it that God created you to do?
- Are you blooming for Christ? Did you balloon with Christ welling within during the pandemic? Pandemic moments are not over. Keep growing. The focus here is the disease of our souls. Pandemic moments are not bad moments. They are just opportunities to develop more intimate intimacy. Is the glass half-full or half-empty? Your perspective matters because it affects your interactions with God and with other people. Look for what God is doing.

YOUR CONVERSATIONS

New retirement, pandemic times, along with a debilitating knee injury, helped me to ponder with God for prolonged periods every day. I found myself developing more intimate intimacy with the Lord. While deadheading blooms, I was looking at two years of balloon plant growth. While sipping coffee after deadheading faded balloon blooms, a snapshot of ministry blossomed. The thought occurred to me that the ministry God gave me focuses on helping others to grow, which was not new. That is my original ministry mandate from the Lord. There I was outside, looking for the design or how to redesign my landscape. The Lord began showing me redesigns, little things in my life, so that I could stay focused and grow my intimacy with a refined mission.

It is not that the mission or the mandate changed. It is not that the assignment changed. God pollinated me with experiences so that whatever stage of intimacy I was in, Creator God could grow me even closer until the day I am called home. Thank you, Lord.

I will shout it from the mountaintop. I want the world to know that the Lord is my everything. From the week I started battling COVID in January 2022, Zion has called me to a higher place of praise. I must not lessen my voice for the Kingdom because someone does not like the volume, the delivery platform, or method, or because their theology cannot accept God's creative way of using me.

As I created this manuscript, I kept saying *shift*. Then, I questioned changing from *shift* to *pollinate*. God refined my calling, redesigned me. God pollinated me. God cross-pollinated me. Cross-pollination is the process of applying pollen from one flower to the pistils of another flower. During the early part of my retirement season as well as COVID recuperation isolation, God acclimated me and I adapted to my next. The Lord let me visualize another way to do ministry in keeping with the same mission. All of it is God allowing me freedom to choose to be continuously shaped, pruned, and have my roots trimmed to blossom more brilliantly.

I set out to redesign the backyard landscape. God had in mind to redesign me, to cross-pollinate my thinking, redesign the ministry rather than change the mission. Listening to the Lord is more important to me than anything in life. I am listening, Lord, as you develop more intimate intimacy. You are growing me in a way that will help me grow other people. Thank you, God. Thank you. You choose to use me, a person who should not even be alive, according to the doctors.

Cross-pollinated and transplanted

Barbara A. F. Brehon

BLOOD

My medical history with blood has been an issue my whole life, and only a couple of years ago I found out about thalassemia. In September 2021, DNA testing indicated that I am "positive for the alpha deletion on both chromosomes." It kept kicking me and I finally had a name for it and a clearer understanding of myself. My niece, who is a pediatrician, helped me to understand what questions to ask the specialist for hematology and oncology. Thalassemia is an inherited blood disorder caused when the body does not make enough hemoglobin. The body's red blood cells do not function properly, and they last shorter periods of time, so there are fewer healthy red blood cells traveling in the bloodstream. Red blood cells carry oxygen to all the cells of the body. When there are not enough healthy red blood cells, a person could feel tired, weak, or short of breath. Severe anemia can damage organs and lead to death.[5]

My blood and the balloon plants' nectar have something in common: Creator God! God transports life-flowing energy through our veins. Without the Lord moving within us, we would not be!

---

[5] https://www.cdc.gov/ncbddd/thalassemia/facts.html   Accessed   on November 7, 2022.

Vibrant veins through which energy flows.

Thalassemia, endometriosis, the blood bubble—there was a time in my life when the gynecologist had me giving him samples of blood every three months so that he could stay on top of whatever would happen that he did not understand. At the time, he knew something was wrong but did not know what it was. I was a young woman having my blood tested routinely but walking around every day like nothing was wrong. Now I have an annual checkup in retirement, and I am finally doing what most people do early in life doing fewer doctor visits than I did when I was in my twenties and thirties. That is God!

New mornings and new mercies I see. *All* I need the Lord has provided. Yes, God waters, grows, and cross-pollinates me. I will continue healthy nutrition to be energized for effective ministry. I cannot do much if I am always physically tired and drained. I am still alive! I am favored by the Father, covered with and by the blood of Jesus even before being placed in my mother's womb, and I am still blooming for Christ.

Keep having conversations with the Lord. Humble yourself before someone else does it for you. The Lord listened to Manasseh because he sought the Lord earnestly and his request moved the Lord (2 Chronicles 33:10–13; 1 Peter 5:6; Nehemiah 4:15–18; Acts 2:17–21).

POINT TO PONDER

Do you position yourself before God with an attitude that makes him want to listen to you?

Lord, I pray for humility in the name of Jesus. Amen

GROW IN GOD-TIME

Wherever life plants you, bloom with grace. Ecclesiastes 3:1–2 says there is a season for everything. Scripture also says that one born of a woman has a few days that are full of trouble, beginning like a flower then withering (Matthew11:11; Psalm 39:5). I feel like these verses describe the season in which I find myself. In "God-time," I am of a few days. I can do things differently to accomplish the same calling refined for such a time as this. I am revitalized after launching the Favored by the Father Ministries digital application available on iOS and Android devices. It is exciting to think that God would use me to reach people all over the world, literally, spewing his word into a cyber sanctuary (Matthew 28:19).

Do I care more about the number on the dashboard's roll or whether I was used saving a soul? Lord, keep me focused on the mission, the assignment, and remind me that the increase is up to *you* (1 Corinthians 3:7).

CHAPTER SIX

SEED SPREADING

W e encounter people wherever we go and, obviously, wherever they are. As we spread seeds along the way, it must be according to God's plan in the gardens of his choice. Otherwise, we might toil endlessly and never see the fruits of our labor. Therefore, we must follow God's directions to select our seeds. Then, we must consider where we are sowing seed and add seed starting mix to our containers. Is it God's plan and place or yours? The Lord may allow you to witness your plants' full transformation into maturity. Make sure you properly start the planting process in prayer for yourself as well as the seeds and the garden.

Rev. BB's Daily Prayer ~ Hover over me, Lord. Forgive me. Be my all in all. Pour over me and into me, Lord. Touch me and seep into every crevice of my life. Work in me and through me each day. Holy Spirit, fill me with your power and wisdom! Leak out of me, Lord. Let others see you at work in my life. Show me your ways, Lord, teach me to trust you more. Help me to be in union with you. Lord, forgive me, and give me a hunger and thirst for you. Lord God, I am not praying for things to get easier, I am praying to become better. I want to crave you and only you. Jesus, give me an overcoming spirit and help me to "speak life" to others in your name. I want to be humble, a powerful lion and yet a meek lamb like Jesus. Help me to be in union with you, Lord. Preserve my relationship with you. I want to be an imprint of your nature. Amen.

Prayer for yourself as well as the seeds makes it easier for sprouts to surface during their growing season. Reference your seed packet, the Lord, for instructions on planting depth and spacing. Giving the person too much information and your insight could stunt his or her growth. Enclose your seeds with a layer of prayer. Keep them covered to lock in whatever God wants to germinate. Keep checking on them; seeds require different conditions like temperature, moisture, and light. [6] Be sure you feed them what the Lord says. Give them words from the Word. Let the Word do the work and pray with/for them—all in a simple conversation with and about Jesus (John 6:22–29). Simple conversations matter.

As soon as your seeds sprout, give them more space but keep taking care of them. While it is important to water your seeds, do not overdo it. The soil must not become oversaturated for delicate seeds. Care for your seedlings with appropriate fertilizing as the Lord instructs, so they are prepared to mature. Too much

---

[6] https://www.masterclass.com/articles/a-guide-to-growing-plants-from-seeds Accessed on 3/3/2023.

of anything can disrupt the growing process, therefore spiritual toughening is needed.

Hardening is part of the process of spreading seeds. Gradual exposure helps prevent falling by the wayside. God will not place more conditions on you than you can bear. You will not experience cold and windy environments without proper protection to endure them. As the seedling is hardier, God puts it in the right garden for its growing season, and new life in Christ.

When your seedlings have adjusted to the new life in Christ, the Lord transplants them to grow more. A Christian does not have to be a baby in Christ to experience new life. New life refers to anyone who has moved to the next level of maturity and more intimate intimacy with the Lord. For example, God let me perceive a different standard making a cell phone application available that became a tool not only for discipleship but also for evangelism. I could see the evangelistic effect after people began downloading and using the application. We reach more people for Christ when we follow the Lord's directions using the available resources.

Mature balloon plant and babies from seeds bursting out.

I attended a conference and heard a vendor speaking about developing a cell phone application that placed ministry essentials under one electronic umbrella. That struck me. I spoke with him individually, and within three months, God let me launch a digital application for Favored by the Father Ministries available for iOS and Android. During the developmental season, I remember a conversation with someone about a podcast, which was not for me to do. Yet, a vendor whom I had never met planted a seed in me that grew.

Our balloons can burst forth exponentially, spreading more seeds than we could ever think possible. Ephesians 3:20 says the Lord is able to do exceedingly and abundantly above all we ask or even think. God makes it all available, so why not use all resources to influence those placed within your reach?

Water the seedlings with the Word of God using platforms, methodology, and resources provided to allow their roots to properly break into their new soil during their growing seasons.

God has the plan for us to plant. We must plant as well as converse with the Lord to ensure that we are in the right field and planting in the right garden. Our omnipresent Savior is always watching us to ensure that we complete the work given to us. When the Lord chooses us to carry a message or to plant seeds, we must fulfill that assignment knowing his watchful eyes are upon us. God is alert and actively paying attention to everything we do. I am grateful that the Lord is with me. When we share the word given to us, it will come true. The Lord will stick with you, observing, watching (Jeremiah 1:12).

God knew our assignment to spread seeds before creating us in the womb. God set us apart and asked us to go to all the nations to proclaim and teach all the things Jesus commanded (Matthew 28:19). God's servants are preordained to carry out particular ministries. Therefore, we must go forth, bloom where we are planted, and continually spread God's seeds.

There is no need to make excuses for not completing the work. Like the people in Jeremiah's time (Jeremiah 1:3–12), we are appointed to serve people who are experiencing difficult times. The Message Bible says that God has holy plans in mind for us. God wants us to proclaim the truth, which has the power to deliver people. Each of us is just the right person with a set of experiences for the people to whom we are sent.

As we bloom for Christ, we balloon or expand and blow out into other people's lives. They recognize God's work. The Holy Spirit expands and blows the breath of life into what we are doing. With our obedient, seed-spreading service, God fertilizes the seed, makes it grow in others' lives, and makes it blossom.

This reminds me that once my young niece wanted to grow some seeds. Years ago, when I was in my early twenties, I remember the time when this curious elementary school child observed that a popcorn kernel was a seed. When I recently asked if she remembered that, she laughed and remembered learning about that in school. Theresa said she thought she was supposed to plant every seed that she saw. She recalled getting her mother to help her plant all kinds of seeds.

She asked my mother if she could grow popcorn and my

mother sternly told her, "No." Seeing the disappointment on her face, I chimed in to encourage her to try it. I assisted her in preparing a disposable cup with soil, water, and planting those seeds, popcorn kernels. We placed it in a kitchen window because she said it needed to get some sun. She nurtured it for a few weeks, and it actually sprouted. The popcorn seed grew to an inch or so, she lost interest, and it wilted.

As we wilt in different growing stages, I am so glad that the Lord does not lose interest in us but continues to nurture us to maturity. Furthermore, it would be incredible if every Christian would want to plant every kernel of faith.

CHAPTER SEVEN

HARVESTING

S ometimes I want so badly to play in the dirt. I simply want to take as much time as I want in my garden. Though it is a pleasant experience, I cannot neglect the heart of the matter. I was so busy documenting bursting my blossoms that I almost missed the magnificent missional message that is climactic to this whole process of blooming for Christ: maturing as a Christian. A mature Christian is God's harvester. In terms of *harvesting* a balloon plant, one removes the pod containing the seeds, perhaps saving them in a brown bag to plant later or in a preferred location to suit a landscape design. However, I must know when to get out of my own garden and go into the field according to the Lord's design.

Jesus told his disciples that the harvest is plentiful, but the laborers are few (Matthew 9:36–38). To that I say, "Lord, I am available. I will bloom where you plant me. I will go whenever and wherever you say, even though loved ones ask, 'Why are you going there?'"

What is a spiritual harvest? John 4:36–42 helps us to understand that the harvest is people brought to eternal life. Many souls need to repent and have faith in Christ. The harvest of human souls will spend eternity somewhere, either heaven or hell. Jesus saw the spiritual harvest of souls awaiting in the Samaritan village and many of them became believers in Christ (John 4:41).

The spiritual harvest is seeing people saved and growing in the Lord. Sometimes we do not see it. Nevertheless, we must not become weary of trying. In due season, we will reap if we persevere (Galatians 6:9). When a Christian perseveres, his or her endurance has a chance to grow and God blesses those with a crown of life (James 1:2, 12; 1 Peter 5:4; 2 Timothy 4:8).

The Lord of the harvest has recruited you and me into his field to harvest these souls on his behalf. The Word of God tells us that some plant, some water, but God provides the increase. The seed sower, the tender, and the reaper are different people at different times (John 4:35–38; 1 Corinthians 3:6–9). Avoid comparing one person's faith to another.

Furthermore, it is not important who does the planting, or who does the watering. What is important is that God makes the seed grow (1 Corinthians 3:7). A spiritual harvest is the result of God's work in individual hearts. The Lord opened Lydia's heart to respond to Paul's message and she shared her faith with others (Acts 16:14, 40).

Let us share our faith and keep *blooming for Christ.*

CONCLUSION

Throughout all stages, God is at work and in charge. Therefore, persevere. Sometimes we become overwhelmed with so much trauma that it is difficult to burst through and burst forth. Then God teaches through the trauma, refines assignments, and we balloon for Christ. We grow more intimate with the Lord. while escorting others to Jesus. As they witness our struggles, they see us emerge through the soil of distress. Consequently, despite what the enemy tries to do to make us wither, we keep growing toward the Son and bloom with grace.

GROWTH STAGES

- Sit where God wants you to sit.
- Move toward the light of the Lord in your growing season. One does not have to shift directions but perceive pivotal modifications to
  - function in discipleship (seed);
  - function as an authentic disciple maker (germination);

- function as an intimately maturing Christian (growth and reproduction);
- function as a bursting balloon for Christ (pollination); and
- function as his means to seed spreading wherever the Lord chooses.

One of my morning message subscribers recently responded with an image that included the phrase, "Wherever God plants, you bloom with grace." I first received it before I fell and fractured my right hand in the season of completing this book. With the Lord's nurturing guidance, I persevered, and the process gave a different meaning to blooming with grace. God's grace is sufficient! Complete the assignment.

God will show you one more piece at a time and will give you provisions despite distractions and hindrances. Our Sovereign Lord may not show you next until you complete now. Why give you more to do if you have not finished the previous assignment? Be faithful in the small things (Luke 16:10).

Trust God's process so that when God gives the signal to go forward, you are prepared and equipped. The process will flow smoothly in God's time. Spend the time needed with whatever the detail is for that moment, that day. It is critical to trust in God for the process, the agenda, and the timing. The Holy Spirit will alert you about spending more or less time on something or whether to bother with it at all. Whenever you ignore that alert, it is on you. Do not charge that to God's account.

Transplanted into the front yard and thriving.

BE TRANSPLANTED AND TRIMMED

God may allow many things to bombard you. Despite the hectic nature of daily life, we must keep focused on what God is directing us to do. It may feel like a disconnect among the many pieces of your puzzle. You might feel uprooted and transplanted in new soil without the appropriate adjustment time, so you are not yet acclimated to a new environment. For whatever reason, you feel like your soil is oversaturated. However, all those things eventually come together. If God had left it up to your devices, you may not have moved.

Respect that your assignment and another person's appointment to serve the Lord are different, but they may run parallel. Keep in mind that any two servants may have similar paths to follow, yet each has his or her own story in different soil and in different gardens.

While you travel the road that you are on, I am traveling on a parallel highway, and we will get to the same destination. Furthermore, every now and then, they will intersect, and we will be blossoming in the same flower garden, sharing our stories, and spreading our seeds. My seed came out of a different package than your seed, yet God planted us in the same garden.

I have been back in my yard gardening and God has been speaking to me. Looking back on many conversations and experiences, I am using the gist of them to know when to post certain things on the Favored by the Father Ministries application for in-depth Bible studies as well as videos. Trusting in God for the process and the details is critical. I decided to follow God's guidance, knowing that everything is not for everyone. I already stepped out of my comfort zone in several arenas since the onset of the COVID pandemic.

Your dream may keep going. The people may keep changing and become faceless. However, the dream reinforces the notion of having a conversation with God all day every day, which is fulfilling. There is no need to be tied up in spiritual knots. Fulfillment is not causing worry nor allowing fret over what someone is doing or not doing. There is peace, though personal sorrow strikes during your growing season. Do not allow it to distract you but use it as an opportunity to reenergize and continue doing and being who and what God has ordained for such a time as this.

Like the balloon plant, Christians grow, blossom, or bloom in phases. It is one plant, yet it is in different phases at the same time.

My mother's note about decay

EPILOGUE

It is amazing that a few weeks after I submitted my manuscript for this book, I came upon a note written in my mother's handwriting while looking for something else. The notes connect growth stages yet take them to another dimension. I do not know whether she had been reading a scripture for personal study, preparing for teaching a Sunday school lesson, or whether she was preparing something for a toastmistress function. However, she clearly stated that when growth stops, decay begins. I immediately thought of mulch and then pondered this point for a few weeks. I knew that I must include it somewhere to conclude *Blooming for Christ*.

Sometimes stunted growth occurs in the process of blooming for Christ. We allow the cares of the world and concerns that other people have deter us and distract us from what we know God told us to do. We become defeated in our own minds having allowed the enemy to reign in our thoughts. We must face the defeats with Christ, who helps us to use life's challenges to escalate and elevate us. In Christ and with Christ we will never be defeated.

Just like I do not want my plants to be deficient and without nutrition, I do not want my spiritual life to be nutrient deficient, either. I thrive with Godly intimacy and desire to use every bit of every day for God's pleasure.

At the end of the plant's growing season, I do not throw away faded blossoms. Add old blooms to a compost pile and allow them to break down for their nutritional value. In a sense this is recycling for free topsoil and mulch. Use compost beneath the top layer of the soil to benefit the soil itself in providing essential nutrients. Use mulch on the top of the soil to control weeds and hold in moisture.[7] Moreover, I replaced grass with rocks to accomplish moisture retention.

As life cycles, there are challenges and approvals, obstacles and advantages, failures, and accomplishments. When we think there is nothing else we can do, we must remember that even decay has purpose. Decay is simply transformation from one state of being to another. Rethink yourself and repurpose your methods. As you become more seasoned and more intimate with God, transformation is constant, and your mindset renews. Romans 12:2 reminds us to conform not to the world. We want to do what is pleasing to God and do the Lord's perfect will in all processes of life, in all seasons of life.

Remember that Genesis 2:7 tells us that God formed humans from the dust of the Earth and blew the breath of life to become a living soul. We will return to dust (Genesis 3:19). In the meantime,

---

[7] https://www.thespruce.com/shredding-leaves-for-use-as-compost-mulch-2130798 Accessed on April 4, 2023.

with every breath we breathe, we humbly and utterly depend on God in whom we live, move and have our being (Acts 17:28).

When life squeezes out all the water from our human structure, we are life-deficient fossils. Similarly, a lifeless leaf without water leaves an outline of what it once was. Yet, that outline provides a method for generations to come to know of Creator God as omnipotent and omniscient throughout the ages. Years of pressure and heat form coal from layers of dirt and rock covered plants. Likewise, diamonds are formed from intense heat and pressure; elements crystallize deep within the Earth. Therefore, humans created from the dust of the ground must be forever mindful that life squeezes us, yet we leave imprints of who God is.

Lasting imprints for God need time to fossilize. We must endure life's challenges, accept them rather than feel defeated, and keep *Blooming for Christ*. Christ is the visible imprint of our invisible God (Colossians 1:15-16).

BIBLIOGRAPHY

"Reasons You Should Shred Leaves for Compost and Mulch." The Spruce. Accessed April 4, 2023. https://www.thespruce.com/shredding-leaves-for-use-as-compost-mulch-2130798

"The Stages of the Flower Life Cycle." Ava's Flowers. Accessed June 17, 2022. https://www.avasflowers.net/the-stages-of-the-flower-life-cycle.

"What happens in the seedling growth stage of germination?" BYJU'S. Accessed March 1, 2023. https://byjus.com/question-answer/what-happens-in-the-seedling-growth-stage-of-germination/.

Barbara Arlene Fields Brehon

ABOUT THE AUTHOR

Rev. Dr. Barbara A. F. Brehon was born and raised in Norfolk, Virginia of the late Richard T. Fields, Sr. and Jerlean W. Fields. As a child, Dr. Brehon found joy and inner peace at her home church, not understanding what it meant to serve the Lord. In her early thirties, she accepted God's call sitting on a beach at a retreat with the Young Adult Ministry. Later, while attending seminary, she recognized her call to equip believers, which is like being a spiritual body builder.

God has majestically interwoven her reading specialist and theological training into creatively sharing his Word for his glory. Laboring for personal intimacy with the Lord, her passion is to help others grow closer to God. She encourages others to recognize their God-gifted purposes and to enjoy the abundance of life in the love of the Lord.

Currently retired and residing in rural Tappahannock, Virginia, Dr. Brehon serves as visionary servant leader of Favored by the Father Ministries (a church without walls) and associate pastor of the Beulah Baptist Church. She is also serving in her second year of a three-year term as moderator of the Southside Rappahannock Baptist Association and Its Allied Ministries, made up of thirty-five churches in Essex, King and Queen, and Middlesex counties in Virginia.

Dr. Brehon preaches and teaches God's Word whenever and wherever called to serve.

Blooming for Christ completes a discipleship trilogy that includes *Reach Me with SMILES: A Handbook for Developing Disciple Makers* and *Beyond Discipleship to Relationship: Developing Intimacy with the Lord*. Each resource offers practical, biblically sound approaches for personal and corporate spiritual growth and are available on her website, www. barbaraafbrehon.com.

As we evolve, we are like butterflies coming out of a box. We allow the Holy Spirit to elevate us to loftier places in the Lord. Thus, the ministry logo emerged.

The design for the Favored by the Father Ministries digital application connects, engages, and helps you grow from wherever you are. We are a church without walls. Features include a daily devotional, prayer requests, Bible Study, multiple Bible versions, and more. Download today.

Remain FAVORED BY THE FATHER.

Download the free digital application for Favored
by the Father Ministries for iOS or Android

Give a donation to Favored by the Father Ministries

Barbara Brehon

Scan to pay $BarbaraBrehon

Give a donation to Favored by the Father
Ministries using Cash App

Printed in the United States
by Baker & Taylor Publisher Services